TAILGATE GEAR

THE ULTIMATE
TAILGATERS COOKBOOK

ISBN: 1-879234-72-6

Published for Dick's Sporting Goods by Dockery House Publishing, Lindale, Texas.

Publisher:	Rodney L. Dockery
Editorial Director:	Caleb Pirtle III
Marketing Director:	Kim Dockery
Art Director:	Jutta Medina
Food Editor/Stylist:	Cole Croghan
Food Photography:	Catrice Tkadlec

First Printing

Manufactured in the United States of America.

The Great Party Outdoors

Tailgating provides a great opportunity to link together those elements that are so important in life: **good food, good drink, good friends, good times, and good memories,** all captured within the unforgettable portals of the great outdoors.

Tailgating has become a traditional part of the American lifestyle, as chefs of all ages gather with their grills and charcoal wherever games are played, car races are run, music filters down from a concert stage, and the rivers are running.

The weather no longer matters. The wind chill may be from ten below in Green Bay to 110 above in South Texas. Party sites range from parks to parking lots and in campgrounds from the side of the American road to the beaches of both rock and sand. They can be found almost anywhere and can't ever be missed.

Just follow the aroma of hickory smoke rising from the grill of a chef who always has a new and different and secret way of taking the same old food and making it taste better than it's ever tasted before.

Ultimate Guide to the Perfect Party

1. Start planning your menu several days in advance, and pack prepared food in disposable containers.

2. Make sure you arrive to a game or event three to four hours early, finding a good place to park. The smart chefs locate a grassy area and often set up shop at the end of a parking row. Such a move gives them room for a serious tailgating party, which generally grows before the afternoon or evening ends.

3. Fly your own personal flag on a pole reaching far above your vehicle so your friends can find you without wasting time walking the whole parking lot. At a ball game, wear your team's colors, and fly the team flags.

4. Food should be ready at least a couple of hours before the game or the event starts. This timetable gives you plenty of time to eat, clean up, and extinguish fires before the referee blows his whistle, an umpire throws out the first pitch, stock car racing drops the checkered flag, or the drummer strikes the first roll.

5. Dress appropriately for the time you spend out of doors, and be prepared for any sudden and dramatic temperature changes. During cold weather, dress in layers, which creates air pockets that lock in the heat and allow you to better retain your own body heat. A hat can lock in body heat as well. As much as 90 percent of your body heat can be lost through the top of your head. The inner layer keeps you dry and comfortable. The middle layer can trap warm air and hold it. The outer layer provides protection from the wind, rain, snow, and other cold weather problems, and the real tailgater never worries about wind, rain, snow, or cold weather ruining a good outdoor party.

6. Don't ever run the risk of running out of food. It can taint your reputation as a tailgate chef forever. It's worth the extra money to have too much food. You can always bring it home or give it away to some unfortunate soul who passes by and doesn't have a tailgate party to attend. New friends are made that way.

7. Bring your food in zip-lock bags. It is far easier and simpler to merely throw the bags away when the party ends than try to start gathering up a bunch of Tupperware containers to haul back home and wash.

8. If you need a pan, invest in a tinfoil pan that can also be thrown away. The life of a genuine tailgater should be as efficient and easy as possible.

9. Bring chairs. Some of your friends, the real pros, will bring their own. But there are always rookies who forget, and standing around on pavement can grow wearisome in a hurry.

10. Bring water. You'll need it to put out the fire, and it always comes in handy when the time comes to start cleaning up.

Gotta' Bring
- ✓ charcoal or propane grill
- ✓ gas or charcoal & lighter fluid
- ✓ portable chairs and tables
- ✓ matches or lighter
- ✓ ice, coolers
- ✓ cooking pans/pots
- ✓ oven mitts, apron
- ✓ trash bags, collapsible trash can
- ✓ bottle opener/can opener/wine opener
- ✓ plates, cups, eating utensils
- ✓ first aid kit
- ✓ plastic storage bags, fire extinguisher
- ✓ umbrella or canopy for too much rain or too much sun
- ✓ kerosene heater, sun block
- ✓ antacids
- ✓ cooking utensil such as a spatula to flip burgers
- ✓ cooking fork to stab franks
- ✓ a good kitchen knife, cutting board
- ✓ a cooking spoon to stir dips
- ✓ plenty of paper towels
- ✓ toothpicks

Don't Forget
- ✓ buns
- ✓ cheese, onions
- ✓ mushrooms, tomatoes
- ✓ lettuce, barbecue sauce
- ✓ salt, pepper, hot stuff
- ✓ ketchup, mayo, mustard
- ✓ pickles
- ✓ Worcestershire sauce
- ✓ salsa and seasonings
- ✓ plenty of water

Ultimate Guide to the Perfect Party

Table Of Contents

Patriot's Beef Short Ribs

Boston Globe

Here's What You Need!

4 to 5 pounds beef short ribs

Steak seasoning for sprinkling

6 cloves garlic, minced

1 medium onion, minced

1 (7 ounce) can chipotles in adobo sauce, seeded and minced, with juice

1 cup ketchup

1 cup maple syrup

1 (12 ounce) bottle of beer

Here's What You're Doing With It!

1. Sprinkle the ribs with steak seasoning, and let them rest for about 10 minutes.
2. Combine the garlic, onion, chipotles, ketchup, maple syrup, and beer in a disposable foil pan, large enough to hold the ribs in a single layer.
3. Over moderately high heat, brown the ribs on the grill, then place them in a single layer, meatier side up, in the foil pan.
4. Push the coals to one side of a charcoal grill, or turn one side of the gas grill off, and set the other side to medium.
5. Place the pan on the cooler side of the grill, and close the grill cover. Maintain just enough heat to keep the liquid barely simmering for about 2 hours, or until the meat is tender.
6. Remove the ribs from the cooking liquid.
7. Skim the layer of grease from the liquid. Place the pan on the hot side of the grill, and boil the liquid until it reduces and thickens.
8. Place the ribs on the cool side of the grill, and baste with the cooking liquid, turning and basting several times.
9. Remove the ribs from the heat, and serve immediately.

Serves 6

Lassen Burger

Here's What You Need!   Shredded beef, enough for four 4-ounce patties

8 slices bread

Spreadable cheese

Here's What You're Doing With It!

1. Form shredded beef into a patty.
2. Grill patties and slices of bread.
3. Places patties on toasted bread.
4. Cover one slice of bread with spreadable cheese.
5. Some say the burger was created by Louis Lassen in New Haven, Connecticut, in 1903, and others say it was introduced at the St. Louis World's Fair in 1904.

50 YARD RUN
DIPS ★ SAUCES ★ BEVERAGES

All-Seasons Spinach Dip

1 bunch kale, washed and tough stems removed

1 bunch spinach, washed and tough stems removed

2 medium cloves garlic, peeled

3 tablespoons toasted pine nuts

4 teaspoons balsamic vinegar

1/2 cup olive oil

1. Bring a large pot of salted water to a boil. Prepare an ice water bath by filling a bowl halfway with ice and water; set aside.
2. Add kale and spinach to the boiling water, and cook until wilted, about 2 minutes. Remove from the boiling water, and plunge into the ice bath. Once the greens are cool, remove from the ice bath, shake off excess water, and place in the bowl of a food processor.
3. Add garlic, pine nuts, and vinegar, and, while pureeing, slowly pour in olive oil. Continue pureeing, stopping to scrape down the sides of the bowl with a rubber spatula as necessary, until all oil is incorporated and the mixture is smooth, about 4 minutes. Season with salt and serve.

SEASONING TIP: Use rubs, marinades, sauces, butters, and bastes to add an extra dimension of flavor. Even something as basic as sea salt and cracked black pepper can really bring out an enriched flavor.

9

Grilled Softshell Crabs

Maine Seafood Connection

Here's What You Need!

12 soft shell crabs, cleaned

1/2 cup olive oil

1/2 cup parsley, fresh, chopped

1 teaspoon lemon juice, fresh

3 tablespoons nutmeg

3 tablespoons soy sauce

1/4 teaspoon Tabasco sauce

Here's What You're Doing With It!

1. In a small bowl, combine olive oil, parsley, lemon juice, nutmeg, soy, and Tabasco sauces.
2. Brush both sides of the soft-shell crabs with the sauce.
3. Place on moderately hot grill about 4 inches from the heat source.
4. Grill until lightly browned on one side, about 5 to 6 minutes.
5. Turn and cook the other side.

Serves 6

Mint Tea Cooler

1 cup boiling water

2 tea bags

2 tablespoons chopped fresh mint

2/3 cup sugar

2/3 cup fresh grapefruit juice

1/2 cup fresh lemon juice

2 cups water

1. Pour boiling water over tea bags and mint leaves. Cover and steep 5 minutes. Strain mixture.
2. Stir in sugar and juices. Serve over crushed ice.
3. Garnish with a fresh mint sprig or lemon wheel.

NORTHEAST

SEAFOOD TIPS: If using marinade on seafood, allow the fish to soak up flavor for at least 30 minutes. Keep cool while soaking in marinade.

NORTHEAST

Red Wine Sauce

1/4 cup dry red wine

1/4 cup red wine vinegar

1/4 cup soy sauce

1/4 cup vegetable oil

2 cloves of garlic, chopped

1 teaspoon cracked black pepper

1. Mix the ingredients in a glass bowl or dish.
2. Use the marinade with chicken or pork.

Beer Brats

6 bratwurst sausages

20 ounces light beer

1 medium onion

Seasoned pepper

3 peeled and sliced garlic cloves

Mustard relish

Cheddar cheese

Hotdog buns

1. Place bratwursts in pot, pour in beer, chopped onion, pepper, and garlic.
   Place pot on grill over flame, and bring to a slow boil for 20 minutes.
2. Remove and grill on low flame heat until browned. You must turn regularly
   to prevent burning.
3. Serve on warm buns, and top with mustard relish and cheese.

Serves 6

GRILLING TIPS: You can spray water on your coals frequently, then cover to capture the smoke. Mesquite, hickory, or oak chips add extra flavor when added to the coals.

Maine Grilled Lobster with Champagne Butter

Maine Seafood Connection

Here's What You Need!

4 fresh lobsters
1 lemon (juice only)
2 sticks butter
2 cups champagne

Here's What You're Doing With It!

1. Place lobster shell side down. Cut body from head to tail with sharp knife, splitting open.
2. Remove heart and intestinal vein.
3. Melt butter in sauce pan, and add lemon juice and champagne.
4. Place split lobster shell side down on grill over medium heat approximately 5 inches from heat source.
5. Brush well with champagne butter mixture, and cook for 8 minutes.
6. Turn lobsters, cook for another 8 minutes.
7. Turn again, brush well with champagne butter mixture, and continue to cook until meat turns opaque.
8. It is best to cook lobsters with top of the grill down.
9. Brush with champagne butter sauce just before serving. The remaining sauce can be used for dipping.

New Hampshire Maple Dogs

Here's What You Need!

4 franks

4 strips of bacon

Maple syrup

Honey mustard

2 cans baked beans

Here's What You're Doing With It!

1. Wrap each frank with a bacon strip.
2. Brush the frank with pure maple syrup while grilling.
3. Dress with honey mustard and baked beans.

Serves 4

14

Neapolitan Burger

Here's What You Need!

Italian herbs

Garlic

Onions

Ground beef for four 4-ounce patties

Mozzarella cheese

Marinara sauce

Crusty bread rolls

Here's What You're Doing With It!

1. Mix Italian herbs, garlic, and onions into ground beef before grilling.
2. Top grilled patties with mozzarella cheese.
3. Dress crusty bread rolls with marinara sauce.

Serves 4

Country Mustard with Garlic Sauce

1/4 cup mustard seeds

1/4 cup red wine

1/3 cup red wine vinegar

1 bay leaf

1/4 cup water

1/4 teaspoon ground allspice

2 teaspoons honey

1/2 teaspoon cracked black pepper

l large clove garlic, minced

1 1/2 teaspoons Kosher salt

1. Combine mustard seeds, red wine, red wine vinegar, and bay leaf in a bowl; let stand 3 to 4 hours at room temperature to soften seeds.
2. Transfer mixture to a food processor or blender. Add water and remaining seasonings. Process or blend mixture until course. Scrape mixture into the top of a double boiler, and stir over simmering water about 10 minutes, or until mustard thickens.
3. Remove bay leaf.

Chef's Note: The mixture will not be as thick as purchased mustard. Place mustard in a jar and cool. Cover and refrigerate.

ADDED FLAVOR TIP: When roasting or grilling with the grill closed, open a can of beer, and place the beer over the hottest part of the fire. The beer will boil and saturate the air inside the pit with water vapor. The technique keeps the roasting meats moist and adds flavor.

Winning Buffalo Wings

Here's What You Need!

2 to 3 pounds chicken wings,
  cut to separate drumettes from
  slender 2-bone parts, tips snipped
  off and discarded.

1 quart buttermilk

1/4 cup Tabasco sauce

1 box (3 1/2 ounces)
  panko crumbs

1 cup dry rub

Cooking oil for grill

Barbecue sauce

Here's What You're Doing With It!

1. Place the wing pieces into a large zip-top plastic bag.
2. In a bowl, mix the buttermilk and Tabasco sauce.
3. Add the liquid to the bag, and reseal.
4. Marinate the chicken for 3 to 4 hours before the big event.
5. At the event, pour the panko crumbs into a shallow dish.
6. Open the bag of marinated chicken. Take out 1 piece at a time, shake off the excess buttermilk (but not too much – it helps the crumbs to stick), and roll in the panko crumbs to coat.
7. Season all of the pieces liberally with dry rub.
8. For a charcoal grill, after the coals are ready, push them to one side of the grill. For a gas grill, turn off one side of the grill. Oil the grate on the cooler side of the grill by pouring cooking oil on a paper towel and, with a pair of tongs, rubbing it on the plate.
9. Grill the chicken pieces in batches on the cooler side of the grill. Otherwise, the coating will burn before the chicken is done.
10. For each batch, cover the grill, and let the wings cook for 20 minutes, then turn them over.
11. Re-cover the grill, and cook another 20 minutes. Use a meat thermometer to determine doneness – 180 degrees.
12. During the last 5 minutes of cooking, apply the barbecue sauce on one side of the wings, and allow it to saturate the panko crumbs.
13. Remove the wings, and serve with extra sauce for dipping.

Chipotle Barbeque Sauce

4 tablespoons vegetable oil

2 onions, minced

8 garlic cloves, minced

8 canned chipotle peppers, seeded
   and minced

1 cup ketchup

1 cup maple syrup

4 cups chicken broth

1/2 teaspoon ground allspice

4 tablespoons fresh lime juice

Salt and pepper, to taste

1. Heat the oil in a large saucepan over medium heat until simmering.
2. Add the onions, and sauté until golden brown.
3. Add the garlic, and cook until fragrant.
4. Stir in peppers, ketchup, maple syrup, chicken broth, and allspice;
    bring to a boil.
5. Season to taste with salt and pepper, and continue to simmer
    until the mixture thickens.
6. Stir in lime juice, and remove from heat.

NORTHEAST

GREAT SAUCE TIP: In order to create a smooth sauce, strain it when the sauce cools.

NORTHEAST

New Jersey Burger
with Beefsteak Tomato

Here's What You Need!

Ground beef for four
4-ounce patties

Mayonnaise

Beefsteak tomato, sliced

Seeded buns

Grilled onions

Eggplant, sliced

Zucchini, sliced

Here's What You're Doing With It!

1. Grill a medium-rare burger, and serve with beefsteak tomato and mayonnaise on a seeded bun.
2. Layer bun with grilled onions, eggplant slices, and zucchini slices.

Serves 4

Hot Crab Dip

6 tablespoons mayonnaise

3 tablespoons Creole mustard

1 tablespoon horseradish cream

1/4 cup minced celery

1/4 cup minced onion

2 teaspoons oregano

Tabasco sauce, to taste

1 pound fresh crabmeat

1 cup coarsely crumbled cornbread

1. Heat oven to 400 degrees, and arrange rack in middle.
2. Combine mayonnaise, mustard, horseradish cream, oregano, celery, and onion until well mixed. Season with salt and Tabasco sauce.
3. Add crab, and mix until well incorporated.
4. Place crab mixture in a 3-cup ovenproof dish, and top with crumbled cornbread. Bake in the oven until golden brown, about 15 minutes.
5. Serve with crackers, toasted bread, or celery sticks.

HAMBURGER TIP: Mixing meats can make a great burger. You can mix three parts beef with one part sausage, or you can add a lamb flavor by mixing equal parts of beef and lamb.

Game Day Beef Kabobs

Here's What You Need!

1/4 cup lemon juice

2 tablespoons Worcestershire sauce

3 tablespoons corn oil

1/3 cup soy sauce

2 tablespoons yellow mustard

1 clove garlic, minced

1 1/2 pounds lean round steak, boneless

1 large green pepper

4 ounces fresh mushrooms

8 cherry tomatoes

1 very large onion

Here's What You're Doing With It!

1. Make marinade by combining lemon juice, Worcestershire sauce, oil, soy sauce, mustard, and garlic.
2. Cut beef into 1-inch chunks, then put in marinade. Cover and marinate in refrigerator for 1 to 3 hours before you head to the tailgate party.
3. Cut vegetables into chunks, making at least 8 pieces of each.
4. Remove beef cubes from marinade, reserving marinade.
5. On 4 medium or long skewers, alternate pieces of meat and vegetables.
6. Grill over hot coals, basting occasionally with marinade, for about 15 minutes, turning skewers regularly.
7. Allow 5 to 10 minutes longer for well-done meat.
8. Serve hot.

Serves 4

Belmont Breeze

3 tablespoons Seagram's 7

3 tablespoons fresh orange juice

3 tablespoons cranberry juice

Juice of 1/2 fresh lemon

1 1/2 tablespoons Harvey's Bristol Cream Sherry

2 tablespoons 7-Up

2 tablespoons club soda

Fresh mint sprigs

1. Shake or stir first five ingredients with 1 cup crushed ice until mixed well.
2. Top with 7-up and club soda.
3. Garnish with mint sprigs.

GRILLING TIPS: Choose lean meats to grill. Less fat means you will have less dripping down into the flames, and that reduces flare-ups.

Maryland Crab Cakes

University of Maryland

Here's What You Need!

1 pound crab meat, pasteurized or fresh

1/2 cup cracker crumbs or bread crumbs

2 eggs

1/4 cup mayonnaise

1 teaspoon seafood seasoning

1/4 teaspoon white pepper

2 tablespoons Worcestershire sauce

1 teaspoon dry mustard

1 slice each minced red and green bell peppers

Peanut oil for frying

Rolls or lettuce leaves.

Here's What You're Doing With It!

1. Carefully remove all cartilage from crab meat.
2. In a bowl, mix together eggs, mayonnaise, seafood seasoning, white pepper, Worcestershire sauce, and dry mustard.
3. Add crab meat; mix evenly and gently.
4. Add cracker crumbs evenly.
5. Add peppers.
6. Shape into 6 cakes.
7. Chill for at least one hour in cold ice chest.
8. Deep fry in oil for 2 to 3 minutes until golden brown.
9. Cool on a plate of paper towels to remove excess grease.
10. Serve on a split roll or on a bed of lettuce.

Serves 6

Coal Town Maple Barbeque Burgers

Northwest Pennsylvania Maple Association

Here's What You Need!

1/2 cup beer

1/3 cup crushed pretzels

3 tablespoons chopped onions

2 tablespoons pickle relish

2 tablespoons salsa

2 teaspoons cayenne pepper

1/2 teaspoon salt

2 pounds ground beef

Maple Barbecue Sauce

Here's What You're Doing With It!

1. Mix beer, pretzels, onions, relish, salsa, cayenne pepper, and salt together, and mix with ground beef.
2. Mold beef into four patties, about inch thick.
3. Grill on medium heat until done, about 15 minutes, turning once.
4. Baste beef patties frequently with Maple Barbecue Sauce until the meat is done, and the sauce has thickened.

MAPLE BARBECUE SAUCE:

1 1/2 cups pure maple syrup

2 tablespoons finely chopped onions

2 1/2 tablespoons chili sauce

2 teaspoons salt

1/4 teaspoon chili powder

1/2 teaspoon dry mustard

1/8 teaspoon pepper

1. Combine all the ingredients and blend well.
2. Makes about 2 cups.

Chesapeake Bean Dip

2 cups canned kidney beans,
   liquid removed

1/2 cup sweet relish

1/2 cup mayonnaise

1 small onion, finely chopped

1 dash Worcestershire sauce

1/2 teaspoon white horseradish

1/8 teaspoon garlic powder

1 pinch dry mustard

Salt and pepper, to taste

1. Rinse the beans, and set them aside to drain.
2. Stir together the relish, mayonnaise, onion, dry mustard, horseradish,
    Worcestershire sauce, garlic powder, salt, and pepper in a medium-sized bowl.

NORTHEAST

GRILLING TIPS: When grilling Hamburgers remember that finely ground meat can become soft and mushy. You will want to use a coarse grind of meat to keep it from falling apart on the grill.

23

Pennsylvania Mushroom Swiss Burger

Here's What You Need!

Ground beef for four 4-ounce patties

Swiss cheese

Onions

Chanterelle and crimini mushrooms

Dijon mustard

Hamburger buns

Salt and pepper, to taste

Here's What You're Doing With It!

1. Grill patties.

2. Saute onion.

3. Melt a generous slice of Swiss cheese on to of each grilled patty.

4. Top each bun with sautéed onions, chanterelle mushrooms, and crimini mushrooms.

5. Serve open-face.

Serves 4

GRILLING TIPS: Apply vegetable spray or rub olive oil onto grill so food does not stick to cooking surface.

Pennsylvania Mushroom Swiss Burger

Chipotle Salsa
Steak

Michigan Department of Agriculture

Here's What You Need!

1 pound round steak, cut to 1-inch thick.

3 tablespoons chopped fresh cilantro

Flour tortillas, warmed

Here's What You're Doing With It!

1. Combine marinade ingredients. Marinate steak in 3/4 cup marinade in refrigerator 6 hours
   or overnight before going to the tailgate party. Refrigerate remaining marinade separately.
2. Remove steak; discard marinade. Place steak on grill over medium, ash-covered coals.
   Grill steak 16 to 18 minutes for medium rare doneness, turning occasionally. Do not overcook.
3. Combine reserved marinade and cilantro. Carve steak. Serve with sauce and tortillas.

Serves 2

Hot & Peppery Corn on the Cob

Here's What You Need!

8 ears corn on the cob

1/2 cup butter, softened

3 tablespoons sliced green onions

1 tablespoon snipped chives

1/4 teaspoon freshly ground black pepper

1/4 teaspoon chili powder

1/4 teaspoon ground white pepper

1/4 teaspoon cayenne pepper

Here's What You're Doing With It!

1. Wrap ears of corn in foil, and cook on the grill for 20 to 30 minutes, or until tender, turning occasionally, then move ears to the other edge of the grid to keep warm.

2. In a small mixing bowl, combine butter, green onions, chives, black pepper, chili powder, white pepper, and cayenne. Mix well.

3. Spread on hot, grilled corn on the cob.

Nebraska Department of Agriculture

KICK OFF

DIPS ★ SAUCES ★ BEVERAGES

MIDWEST

EXTRA FLAVOR TIP: To infuse flavor in your grilling, place chunks of onion, garlic, or hot peppers into a heavy foil packet with olive oil. Cooking them slowly allows the aroma to transfer to the meat.

Grilled Beef Steak And Colorful Peppers

Iowa Department of Agriculture

Here's What You Need!

2 well-trimmed beef Porterhouse or T-Bone steaks, cut 1-inch thick

2 small red, yellow, or green bell peppers, cut into quarters.

Parsley Pesto:

1/2 cup packed fresh parsley leaves

4 large cloves garlic, minced

3 tablespoons olive oil

Here's What You're Doing With It!

1. Place pesto ingredients in small bowl of food processor or blender container. Cover; process until parsley is finely chopped, stopping and scraping side of bowl as needed.
2. Spread pesto generously on both sides of steaks and bell peppers.
3. Place steaks and bell peppers on grid over medium, ash-covered coals. Grill, uncovered, 14 to 16 minutes for medium rare to medium doneness and until peppers are tender, turning occasionally.
4. Remove bone and carve steaks into slices.
5. Season with salt and pepper, as desired.
6. Serve beef with bell peppers.

Serves 4

28

Ozark Barbeque Baste

1/2 stick butter, melted

1/2 cup grape juice

1 clove garlic, crushed

1 teaspoon thyme

1 teaspoon basil

1. Mix all ingredients together.
2. Baste while grilling chicken, beef, fish, or pork.

GRILLING TIPS: Know when your steak is done. Medium rare is 145 degrees, medium 160 degrees, and well done 170 degrees.

Barbecue Burgers

Here's What You Need!

1 pound ground beef

1 pound ground turkey

1/2 cup seasoned bread crumbs

1 (8 ounce can) barbecue sauce

1 cup grated Cheddar cheese

Lettuce, tomatoes, sliced pickles, to garnish

Here's What You're Doing With It!

1. In bowl, combine ground beef, ground turkey, bread crumbs, and sauce.
2. Form into patties.
3. Grill over medium hot coals until done.
4. Top with grated cheese.
5. Add lettuce, tomatoes, pickles, and more sauce to taste.

Serves 6-8

MIDWEST

GRILLING TIPS: When you grill a beef patty for hamburgers, a lot of the fat will drain off. If you start with a lean patty, the patty will be too dry. The patty that's 30 percent fat, however, will shrink only 25 percent.

Barbecue Burgers

South Dakota Department of Agriculture

Barbeque and Mustard Glazed Pork Roast

Missouri Department of Agriculture

Here's What You Need!

1 (12 ounce) bottle barbecue sauce

2 tablespoons finely grated orange peel

1/4 cup fresh orange juice

1/4 cup mustard

1/2 teaspoon ginger

1/2 teaspoon salt

1/4 teaspoon cayenne pepper

4 pounds pork loin roast, tied

Apple wood chips to grill

Here's What You're Doing With It!

1. In a small bowl, combine first 7 ingredients; set aside.
2. Pre-heat grill for indirect cooking.
3. Place wire rack 4 to 6 inches over drip pan. Place roast on rack.
4. Cover grill; open vents slightly.
5. Cook roast 45 minutes and turn.
6. Add briquets and chips to fire as needed.
7. Baste with glaze every 10 minutes.
8. Cook for another 45 minutes, or until pork has a slight tinge of pink when cut at thickest part.
9. Remove from grill, wrap in plastic film, and let stand for 10 minutes.

Beer Cheese Dip

1 (16 ounce) package processed cheese spread, softened

1 (8 ounce) package cream cheese, softened

2 tablespoons herb dip mix

3/4 cup beer

Assorted crackers

1. Combine and heat cheese spreads, cream cheese, dip mix, and beer.
2. Add more beer if a thinner consistency is desired.
3. When thoroughly heated, serve with crackers.
4. Makes 3 cups.

MIDWEST

GRILLING TIP: When grilling pork, the meat should be three to six inches away from the heat source. Grilling over high heat shortens the cooking time but toughens the pork.

33

Tex-Mex Chicken

Here's What You Need!

1/2 cup milk

1 cup yellow corn meal

4 tablespoons picante sauce

1 (3-31/2 pound) whole chicken, cut in pieces

1/4 cup melted butter or margarine

Here's What You're Doing With It!

1. Pour milk into pie plate.
2. On waxed paper, combine corn meal and picante sauce; mix well.
3. Dip chicken pieces into milk, then into corn meal mixture, coating all sides.
4. Cover the grill with foil, then place chicken on it.
5. Grill 30-45 minutes, turning twice.

Serves 6

Classic Nacho Dip

1/2 cup chopped onion

2 tablespoons margarine

1 pound processed cheese spread, cubed

1 (8 ounce) can chunky salsa

2 tablespoons cilantro, chopped

Tortilla chips

1. Saute onions in margarine; reduce heat to low.
2. Add remaining ingredients; stir until process cheese spread is melted.
3. Serve hot with tortilla chips or vegetables
4. Yields three cups

MIDWEST

CAUTION: Chicken needs to cook until the meat is no longer pink inside.

Prize Grilled Turkey Steaks

Here's What You Need!

5 cups white wine

1/4 cup soy sauce

1 tablespoon vegetable oil

1 clove garlic, mashed, or

1/4 teaspoon garlic powder

1 pound turkey breast steaks, 1-inch thick

Here's What You're Doing With It!

1. Before going tailgating, combine wine, soy sauce, oil, and garlic in glass dish.
2. Add turkey breast steaks, turning to coat both sides.
3. Cover and marinate in refrigerator at least 2 hours.
4. Turn steaks in marinade several times.
5. At the tailgate party, grill drained turkey steaks over medium hot coals 5-7 minutes per side, basting with marinade a couple of times.

Serves 3 - 4

Berry Apple Bliss

2 cups boiling water

8 blackberry herb tea bags

2 cups apple juice

4 cups ice cubes

2 (12 ounce) cans lemon/lime seltzer

Ice

1.   Pour boiling water over tea bags, and steep 5 minutes; remove tea bags.

2.   Add apple juice, cold water, ice, and lemon/lime seltzer.

3.   Serve over ice.

4.   Serves 11-14.

EXTRA FLAVOR TIP: If you want to infuse your chicken with a better flavor, rub your butter, seasonings, or herbs under the skin. Seasonings can't penetrate the skin, and you lose a great deal of your flavor.

Grilled Dakota Walleye

Iowa Department of Agriculture

Here's What You Need!

- 1/3 cup black or mixed peppercorns
- 1 teaspoon coriander seeds
- 2 tablespoons coffee beans
- 1 tablespoon cilantro
- 1 teaspoon salt
- 4 walleyed pike
- 1 1/2 cups red wine
- 1/4 cup barbecue sauce
- 1/4 cup soy sauce
- 2 cloves garlic, crushed
- 2 teaspoons paprika

Here's What You're Doing With It!

1. In a spice grinder or pepper mill, grind pepper, coriander seeds, and coffee beans.
2. Add salt and cilantro.
3. Compress spice mixture onto both sides of steaks; place into large plastic food bags.
4. Combine wine, barbecue sauce, soy sauce, garlic, and paprika. Pour over fish.
5. Close bags and refrigerate several hours before the tailgate party.
6. Turn fish twice while it marinates. Reserve about 1/2 cup of the marinade for grilling.
7. Remove walleye from marinade and pat dry with paper towels.
8. At the tailgate party, preheat grill to medium heat.
9. Grill walleyes over medium coals to desired doneness, allowing 10-15 minutes per side.
10. Brush with marinade as they cook.

Serves 4

Fiesta Beef Dip

1 pound ground beef

1 medium onion, chopped

1 (6 ounce) can tomato paste

1 (8 ounce) can tomato sauce

1 1/2 cups shredded Cheddar cheese

1 (4 ounce) can chopped green chilies, drained

Tortilla chips

1. Cook ground beef and onion until meat is browned; drain.
2. Blend in remaining ingredients, and heat until cheese melts.
3. Serve warm with chips.
4. Makes 4 cups.

Summer Rum Punch

1 1/2 cups rum

1/3 cup banana liqueur

1 dash grenadine syrup

1 (6 ounce) can frozen orange juice concentrate

1 (6 ounce) can frozen pineapple juice concentrate

1 orange, sliced into rounds

1 lime, sliced into rounds

1 lemon, sliced into rounds

1. In a large punch bowl, prepare the orange and pineapple juice according
   to package directions.
2. Stir in the rum, banana liqueur and Grenadine.
3. Float slices of orange, lime and lemon on top.

EASY CLEAN UP TIP: A grill basket makes grilling fish or veggies considerably easier for cooking and clean- up. You can spray or coat the basket with oil to prevent sticking.

Garlic-Parmesan Burgers

Here's What You Need!

2 pounds ground beef

1/2 cup grated Parmesan cheese

1/4 cup minced green onions

2 teaspoons minced garlic

Salt and pepper, to taste

4 slices sourdough bread, cut 1/2-inch thick

Olive oil

Tomato Relish:

3 cups chopped red tomatoes

2 cups chopped yellow tomatoes

1/4 cup thinly sliced fresh basil

1 teaspoon minced garlic

1/2 teaspoon salt

1/2 teaspoon pepper

Here's What You're Doing With It!

1. Combine tomato relish ingredients in medium bowl and set aside.
2. Combine ground beef, cheese, green onions, and garlic in medium bowl, mixing lightly but thoroughly. Lightly shape into eight 1/2-inch thick patties.
3. Place patties on grid over medium, ash-covered coals. Grill, uncovered 11 to 13 minutes to medium doneness, until not pink in center and juices show no pink color, turning occasionally.
4. Season patties with salt and pepper.
5. Meanwhile, brush both sides of bread slices with oil. About 3 minutes before burgers are done, place bread on grid. Grill until lightly toasted, turning once.
6. Place 1 burger on each bread slice, top each with 1/4 cup tomato relish. Serve open-faced.

Serves 8

CAUTION: If you use marinade as an extra sauce on top of cooked fish, the marinade liquid must be boiled by itself for at least 5 minutes to cook out any bacteria that my be left over from the time the fish was soaking.

Garlic-Parmesan
Burgers

Flat Iron Steaks

4 beef shoulder top blade
  (flat iron) steaks
6 ears freshly sweet corn, in husks
2 tablespoons butter, softened
1 teaspoon fresh lime juice
1 medium poblano pepper
1 small red chili pepper or
  Serrano pepper
Lime wedges
Salt and ground black pepper

Rub:
2 tablespoons ground cumin
3 large cloves garlic, minced
2 teaspoons brown sugar
1/2 teaspoon freshly grated
  lime peel
1/4 teaspoon ground
  red pepper

Here's What You're Doing With It!

1. Pull back husks from corn, leaving husks attached. Remove and discard corn silk. Bring husks back up around corn; tie in place with kitchen string or strips of corn husk. Soak corn in cold water at least 10 minutes.

2. Combine rub ingredients. For cumin-lime butter, combine 2 teaspoons rub mixture, butter and lime juice in small bowl; set aside. Press remaining rub evenly onto beef steaks. Cover and place in ice chest to keep refrigerated for 30 minutes.

3. Remove corn from water. Place on grid over medium, ash-covered coals. Grill, uncovered 20 to 30 minutes until tender, turning occasionally. About 15 minutes before corn is done, move ears to outer edge of grill. Place poblano and chili pepper in center of grid; grill poblano pepper 10 to 15 minutes and chili pepper 5 minutes, or until skins are completely blackened, turning occasionally. Place peppers in plastic bag, set aside.

4. Place steaks on grid over medium, ash-covered coals. Grill, covered, 10 to 14 minutes for medium rare to medium doneness, turning occasionally.

5. Remove and discard husks from corn. Spread cumin-lime butter over corn.

6. Carve steaks into slices. Squeeze lime wedges over steaks. Season beef and corn with salt and black pepper.

Serves 6 to 8

Butter Barbecue Sauce

1/4 cup butter

1/4 cup chopped onion

1 cup barbecue sauce

4 teaspoons fresh lemon juice

1 tablespoon Worcestershire sauce

1 teaspoon brown sugar

1/2 teaspoon dry mustard

1/4 teaspoon salt

1. Melt butter in a small saucepan; sauté onion until tender.
2. Add remaining ingredients; mix well.
3. Simmer, uncovered, 10 minutes.
4. Makes 1 1/2 cups.

MIDWEST

STEAK TIP: Tongs enable you to turn the steak without stabbing it. If you stab the steak while grilling, it will begin to lose its rich juices.

Barbecue
Ribs

Barbecue Ribs

Here's What You Need!

6-8 pork rib slabs
1/2 teaspoon salt
1/2 teaspoon pepper
1 (18 ounce) bottle barbecue sauce

Here's What You're Doing With It!

1. Before the tailgate party, place rib slabs in 9- X 13-inch cake pan.
   Salt and pepper; cover pan with foil.
2. Bake in 300-degree oven for 3 hours, or until tender.
3. At the party, place rib slabs on hot charcoal grill approximately 10 minutes on each side.
4. Turn ribs; baste generously with sauce.
5. Grill 1-2 minutes before turning ribs.
6. Baste.

Serves 6-8

MIDWEST

SAUCE TIP: When using barbecue sauce, wait until the meat is almost done before brushing on the sauce. If cooked too long, the sauce will burn and turn black.

Georgia Veggie Burger

Here's What You Need!

Eggplant

Onions

Bell Peppers

Mushrooms

2 tablespoons flour

1 egg.

Mozzarella cheese

Fresh basil

Creamy Italian dressing

Hamburger buns

Here's What You're Doing With It!

1. Combine chopped eggplant, onions, bell peppers, and mushrooms with flour and 1 egg (for each patty).
2. Grill and top with melted mozzarella cheese, fresh basil, and dressing.

Pepperoni Dip

1 can cream of chicken

1 (8-inch long) pepperoni stick, chopped up into little squares

1 square package cream cheese

1. Mix ingredients together.
2. Heat on top of stove until the mixture starts to boil.

Southern Cider

2 quarts apple cider

1/4 cup packed brown sugar

18 teaspoons ground ginger

1 orange, unpeeled

2 cinnamon sticks

1 teaspoon whole cloves

Brandy

1. Combine cider, sugar, ginger, and orange in slow cooker.
2. Tie cinnamon and cloves in a small cheesecloth bag; add to crockpot.
3. Cover and cook on LOW 2 to 4 hours.
4. Remove the bag of spices.
5. Place a shot of brandy in a mug, then fill with hot mix from the cooker.

Makes 10 to 12 servings

GRILLING TIPS: Grill beef, pork, and vegetables about four inches from the heat source, chicken about six to eight inches away.

Barbecue Prawns with Fresh Corn Relish

Here's What You Need!

1/2 cup sour cream

1/2 teaspoon hot sauce

2 tablespoons freshly squeezed lime juice

3 cups fresh corn kernels, cooked

1 small red onion, diced

1 jalapeño pepper, seeded and finely diced

2 plum tomatoes, peeled, seeded, and diced

2 tablespoons cider vinegar

3/4 cup olive oil, divided

1 tablespoon chopped cilantro

Salt and freshly ground black pepper

18 prawns

1/2 cup barbecue sauce

6 cups mesclun greens

Here's What You're Doing With It!

1. Combine sour cream, hot sauce, and lime juice in a small bowl, then set aside.
2. In a separate bowl, toss together corn, onion, jalapeño, tomatoes, vinegar, olive oil (minus 2 tablespoons) and cilantro to create corn relish. Season to taste with salt and pepper, then set aside.
3. Thread the length of the prawns on skewer. Season lightly with salt and pepper.
4. Brush with remaining 2 tablespoons olive oil.
5. Place on hot grill for 30 seconds. Brush with barbecue sauce, and grill for 30 seconds longer.
6. Turn prawns over, and brush with more barbecue sauce. Grill for 1 minute. Remove prawns from grill, and cool lightly.
7. To serve, toss mesclun greens with some of the liquid from corn relish.
8. Place a mound of greens in center of each plate. Arrange prawns over lettuce. Spoon corn relish in a band across prawns, and drizzle with dressing.
9. Serve immediately.

Serves 4

48

Southern Molasses
Barbecue Sauce

3 cups chicken stock

2 cup dry white wine

1/4 cup apple cider vinegar

1/4 cup light molasses

1/4 cup chopped fresh tomato

3 tablespoons minced onions

2 tablespoons chipped pitted dates

1 tablespoon chopped garlic

1/2 teaspoon black cracked pepper

1. Mix all ingredients together, using a large saucepan.
2. Bring to a boil, and reduce to 1 1/2 cups until it has thickened. Stir while reducing.

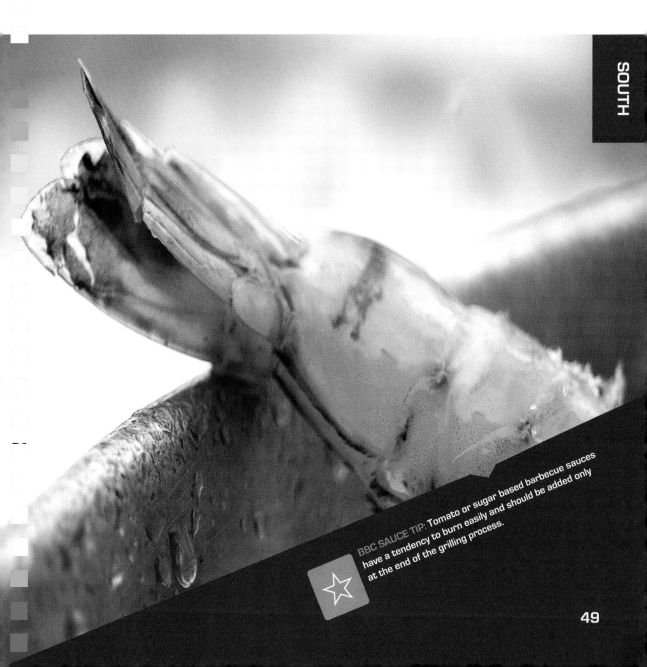

BBC SAUCE TIP: Tomato or sugar based barbecue sauces have a tendency to burn easily and should be added only at the end of the grilling process.

Grilled Steak and Vegetable Pizza

Here's What You Need!

2 packages deep pan pizza crust mix

1/4 pound boneless sirloin steak, cut 3/4-inch thick

2 tablespoons corn meal

3 tablespoons olive oil

1 small eggplant (6 to 7 inches long), cut crosswise into
1/2-inch-thick slices

1 large yellow bell pepper, quartered

2 medium plum tomatoes, very finely sliced

1 cup (4 ounces) shredded smoked Gouda cheese

Chef's Note: May substitute mushroom, zucchini, or yellow squash for vegetables.

Here's What You're Doing With It!

1. Sprinkle corn meal on 2 large baking sheets. Combine pizza crust mixes in large mixing bowl; add 1 cup hot water, and prepare according to package directions.

2. Divide dough into 4 pieces. Place on corn meal coated pans; roll or press out into free form rectangles, about 3- X 5-inches. Brush lightly with some of the oil. Cover with plastic wrap, and keep cold in ice chest.

3. Brush eggplant and bell pepper with oil.

4. Grill vegetables and steak, uncovered over medium heat about 13-16 minutes, or until steak is medium rare to medium doneness, and vegetables are tender. Turn occasionally.

5. Remove steak and vegetables from grill to cutting board.

6. Cut eggplant slices into quarters while grill is cooling to medium-low heat.

7. Cut bell pepper pieces into thin strips, and carve steak crosswise into thin slices.

8. Place pizza crusts, corn meal sides down, directly on grid. Grill two batches if necessary.

9. Grill, uncovered, 3 to 4 minutes, or until bottom is brown.

10. Turn crusts over. Arrange one-fourth of the eggplant, tomatoes, beef, and bell pepper on each crust; sprinkle with cheese.

11. Grill, covered, 2 to 3 minutes, or until crusts are browned on bottom, and cheese is softened. (Cheese does not melt completely.)

12. Watch carefully so the crusts do not burn; rotate pizzas as necessary.

Makes 4 pizzas

FIRE TIP: Use lump charcoal because it is clean, pure, and burns hotter, thereby producing less ash in the bottom of your grill.

SOUTH

Grilled Steak and Vegetable Pizza

Kentucky Department of Agriculture

Taco Dip

1 package cream cheese

1 package taco seasoning

1 small tub sour cream

Mexican cheese

1. Mix cream cheese, taco seasoning, and sour cream together.
2. Top with shredded Mexican cheese.
3. Serve with tortilla chips.

Touchdown Twisters

6 ounces cheese, softened

8 ounces sour cream

5 whole green onions, chopped

4 ounces chopped green chilies, drained

1/2 cup shredded sharp Cheddar cheese

2 tablespoons chopped black olives

12 large flour tortillas

8 ounces salsa

1. In a food processor, combine cream cheese, sour cream, green onions, chilies, Cheddar cheese, and olives. Process until smooth.
2. Spread mixture on tortillas.
3. Roll up each tortilla tightly.
4. Wrap tortillas individually in damp paper towels. Place in airtight plastic bag. Keep refrigerated until ready to serve.
5. Remove tortillas from plastic bags and paper towels. Slice each rolled tortilla crosswise into 1-inch pieces. Place a toothpick in each, and serve with a bowl of salsa on the side for dipping.

Makes 5-dozen pieces

Chef's Note: These can be made ahead and carried to the event in an ice chest.

MARINADE TIPS: Marinades can also tenderize meats. To do so, a marinade must contain an acidic ingredient. You can use lemon juice, vinegar, yogurt, wine or salsa. The enzymes found in fresh pineapple, papaya and ginger also work as natural tenderizers.

Country Grilled Bass

Here's What You Need!

1/4 cup soy sauce

2 tablespoons sugar

1 tablespoon garlic, finely minced

1 tablespoon green onion, finely minced, green part only

2 tablespoons oil

2 tablespoons sesame seeds

4 bass filets, skin on (about 2 pounds)

Here's What You're Doing With It!

1. Combine soy sauce, sugar, garlic, green onion, and oil; set aside.
2. Place sesame seeds in a medium frying pan, and stir over medium heat atop the grill until they begin to brown. They brown quickly, so watch carefully. Add to soy sauce mixture.
3. Cut each filet into 2 pieces. Lay filets skin down in a single layer in a pan with raised sides.
4. Pour soy sauce mixture over filets. Let sit for a moment, then turn filets so they are flesh side down. Cover and keep cold in ice chest for 30 minutes.
5. When ready to grill, remove from marinade, and place bass on oiled grill over ashen coals, skin side touching the grill.
6. Grill for 3 to 4 minutes on one side only. Do not turn filets or they will fall apart.
7. Baste filets with marinade every minute or so until done.
8. Use a greased spatula to transfer fish to plates.

Serves 4

Virginia Aristocrat Burger

Here's What You Need!

Pepper Jack cheese

Fresh ground round, enough
  for four 4-ounce patties

Seeded hamburger buns

Mayonnaise

Cracked black pepper

Crisp bacon

Black olive slices

Avocado slices

Broccoli sprouts

Here's What You're Doing With It!

1. Melt Pepper Jack cheese on top of a grilled patty.
2. Spread seeded buns with mayonnaise, and sprinkle with cracked black pepper.
3. Garnish with crisp bacon, black olive slices, avocado slices, and broccoli sprouts.

Mint Julep

3 cups water

2 cups powdered sugar

1/2 cup roughly chopped fresh mint leaves

52 ounces bourbon

8 sprigs fresh mint leaves for garnish

1. Combine water, sugar, and chopped mint leaves in a small saucepan. Bring to a boil over high heat until the sugar is completely dissolved.
2. Allow syrup to cool approximately 1 hour. Pour syrup through a strainer to remove mint leaves.
3. Fill 8 cups with crushed ice, and pour four ounces of bourbon and 1/4 cup mint syrup into each. Top each cup with a mint sprig.

Serves 8

Kickoff Cocktail

2 ounces rum

1 ounce fresh lime juice

2 ounces fresh orange juice

1 teaspoon Tabasco pepper sauce

1 teaspoon grenadine

Soda water

Orange slice

1. Combine rum, lime juice, orange juice, and Tabasco sauce in a tall glass filled with ice. Stir well.
2. Pour grenadine over top, and fill glass with soda water. Stir gently.
3. Serve with orange slice on the rim of the glass.

Makes 1 serving

Chef's Note: Grenadine is a sweet, dark syrup fashioned from pomegranates.

CAUTION: Burning or overcooking garlic will give your sauce a nutty flavor, rather than the garlic taste you really want.

Grilled Catfish with Crimson Tide Salsa

Georgia Beef Council

Grilled Catfish with Crimson Tide Salsa

Here's What You Need!

4 catfish filets, 6 to 8 ounces each

6 tablespoons (3/4 stick) unsalted butter

2 teaspoons Dijon mustard

Crimson Tide (strawberry) Salsa:

2 cups ripe strawberries, hulled and chopped

2 tablespoons fresh mint leaves, chopped

2 tablespoons sugar

2 tablespoons dark rum

1/2 teaspoon freshly ground black pepper

Here's What You're Doing With It!

1. In a small saucepan, held over the grill, melt the butter and whisk in the mustard.
2. When ready to grill, place an oiled grill rack over the fire. Lightly baste each side of the fish with the mustard butter, and place on the rack.
3. Grill until opaque and just beginning to flake when tested with a fork, 4 to 5 minutes per side, turning once halfway through the grilling time.
4. Baste frequently with the mustard butter.
5. Serve with salsa on the side.

Serves 4

For Crimson Tide Salsa:

1. In a small bowl, combine the ingredients.

Yield 2 cups

GRILLING FISH TIP: Fish has a tendency to dry out and break into small pieces, but you can brush on fresh lemon juice to keep the meat moist and enhance the flavor.

America's Favorite Pork Chops

Here's What You Need!

4 pork chops, about 3/4-inch thick
3/4 cup Italian dressing
1 teaspoon Worcestershire sauce

Here's What You're Doing With It!

1.   Place all ingredients in a self-sealing bag, and keep cold in ice chest for at least 20 minutes.
2.   Remove chops from bag, discarding marinade.
3.   Grill over medium-hot fire, turning once, until just done, about 8 to 11 minutes total cooking time.

Serves 4

Buffalo Chicken Dip

Chicken strips
1 package cream cheese
1 small bottle of ranch dressing
1 small bottle of red hot
Cheddar cheese, grated
Tortilla chips
Celery

1.   Boil chicken Strips, then chop very fine.
2.   Melt cream cheese, ranch dressing, and red hot together, then add chicken.
3.   Top with shredded Cheddar cheese, and bake in the oven at 350 degrees for 30 to 45 minutes.
4.   Serve with tortilla chips and celery.

EASY CLEAN UP TIP: Keep your grill clean by brushing the grate before and after every grilling. You should oil the grate to prevent food from sticking.

SOUTH

Plantation Style Grilled Pork

Alabama Tourism Department

Here's What You Need!

4 pork chops, 1 1/2-inch thick

1/3 cup cider vinegar

1/2 cup molasses

1/2 cup prepared mustard

3 tablespoons Worcestershire sauce

1/2 teaspoon crushed red pepper flakes

Here's What You're Doing With It!

1. Place chops in self-sealing plastic bag.
2. In small bowl, stir together remaining ingredients, and pour over chops.
3. Seal bag and let stand for one hour.
4. Remove chops from marinade, discarding remaining marinade.
5. Grill over a medium-hot fire for 12 to 15 minutes, turning as necessary to brown evenly.

Serves 4

Grilled Fish Tacos

Tennessee Department of Agriculture

Here's What You Need!

2 pounds fresh grouper, snapper, or mahi-mahi filets

8-12 flour tortillas, soft

1 head shredded lettuce

Marinade:

2 tablespoons olive oil

2 tablespoons garlic, minced

1 teaspoon cumin

1 teaspoon chili powder

2 tablespoons lime juice

Here's What You're Doing With It!

1. Combine fish filets with marinade mixture, and keep cold in ice chest for 1 hour.
2. Grill filets on a hot grill.
3. Chop cooked filets into bite-sized pieces.
4. Fill tortilla with shredded lettuce, fish pieces, and Mango Avocado Salsa.

Serves 4

Mango Avocado Salsa:

2 mangos, diced medium

1 avocado, diced medium

1/4 cup red onion, diced

1 tablespoon jalapeño pepper, minced

2 tablespoons cilantro, chopped

1 tablespoon lime juice

1 tablespoon olive oil

Salt and pepper, to taste

1. Combine all ingredients.
2. Mix well and keep cold in ice chest until ready to use.

Southern Secrets
Barbecue Sauce

3/4 cup black cherry soda
1 (17 ounce) can cherries, drained
1/4 cup dry red wine
3 tablespoons cherry jam
2 tablespoons lemon juice
2 tablespoons butter
1 tablespoon brown sugar
2 tablespoons cornstarch
1/2 teaspoon ground cinnamon
Salt and pepper, to taste

1. Combine 1 tablespoon of wine with the cornstarch, and mix until it forms an even paste; set aside.
2. Combine remaining ingredients in a saucepan, and bring to a low boil. Reduce heat and simmer for 5 minutes, stirring.
3. Add the cornstarch paste, and return the sauce to a boil, stirring constantly. Allow to boil until the sauce thickens.
4. Remove from heat and allow to cool.

SOUTH

FLAVOR TIP: If your grill has a top, close it to allow smoke to add its own unique flavor.

Popper Beef Burgers

SOUTH

Here's What You Need!

1 pound ground beef

1/4 cup prepared thick-and-chunky salsa

4 Cheddar cheese-stuffed jalapeño peppers

1/4 cup prepared salsa con queso

1/4 cup chopped fresh plum tomato

2 tablespoons sliced pitted ripe olives

prepared thick-and-chunky salsa

Hamburger buns

Here's What You're Doing With It!

1. Combine ground beef and 1/4 cup salsa in large bowl, mixing lightly but thoroughly. Lightly shape into four thin patties.
2. Place one stuffed pepper in center of each patty; wrap beef around pepper to enclose, sealing seams and forming ball.
3. Flatten balls into patties. Patties will be about 4 to 5 inches across and 1-inch thick.
4. Place patties on grill over medium, ash-covered coals.
5. Grill, uncovered, 15 to 16 minutes to medium doneness, until beef is not pink in center, and juices show no pink color, turning occasionally.
6. Spread 1 tablespoon salsa con queso evenly over top of each burger.
7. Sprinkle evenly with tomato and olives.
8. Serve with salsa.
9. Serves 4.

Cooking Tip: Four slices (3/4 ounce each) Mexican-style process cheese may be substituted for salsa con queso. Place on top of patties 1 minute before patties are done to allow cheese to melt. Popper burgers should be served in hamburger buns.

SMOKING TIP: If you use wood chips, soak them in water for 30 to 60 minutes. If using wood chunks, soak in water for 2 to 3 hours.

Popper
Beef Burgers

Santa Cruz Tacos

Oklahoma Department of Agriculture

Here's What You Need!

1 pound ground beef

1/2 onion, chopped

1/2 cup chili paste

2 teaspoons chili mix

1 teaspoon salt

1 dozen taco shells

Grated Longhorn cheese

Shredded lettuce

Chopped tomatoes

Picante sauce

Here's What You're Doing With It!

1. Brown ground beef in large skillet.
2. Stir in onions, and sauté until tender.
3. Add chili paste, salt, and chili mix; stir to mix well.
4. Cover skillet, cook over low heat 10-15 minutes.
5. Fill taco shells with meat mixture.
6. Garnish with grated cheese, shredded lettuce, chopped tomatoes, and picante sauce.

Serves 4 - 6

Shotgun Willie's Bloody Mary

Bloody Mary Mix

Tequila, gin, vodka, or rum

Ice

Celery stalks

Lime slices

Stuffed olives

1. Combine 3-4 parts Bloody Mary Mix and 1 part of the choice of spirits.
2. Pour the liquid into glasses over ice and stir.
3. Garnish with celery stalks and lime slices.
4. As a finishing touch, sink a stuffed olive into the Bloody Mary just before serving.

SLAM DUNK

DIPS ★ SAUCES ★ BEVERAGES

Frijoles Y Queso Con Guacamole

Frijoles Y Queso Con Guacamole

1 (16 ounce) can refried beans

2 ripe avocados, pureed

1 cup sour cream

1 cup mild cheddar cheese

1 (2.25 ounce) can ripe sliced olives

1 cup chopped cilantro

1 jar hot or mild salsa

Tortilla chips

1. Spread beans over large platter, 1/4-inch thick; pour avocado on top.
2. Spread sour cream over avocado, being careful not to blend.
3. Sprinkle thin layer cheese over sour cream, then olives. Sprinkle cilantro on top.
4. Spread salsa 1/4-inch thick.
5. Serve with tortilla chips.

Serves 6-8

SAUCE TIP: Cooking your sauce with a low heat over time is better than cooking it quickly on high heat.

Steak Tino

Here's What You Need!

10 cloves garlic, quartered

1 (4 pound) thick sirloin

4 tablespoons pepper

2 cups white wine

5 tablespoons loose leaf basil

2 tablespoons stone ground mustard

1/2 cup olive oil

3 tablespoons salt

Here's What You're Doing With It!

1. Insert clove quarters in sirloin.
2. Mix together next 6 ingredients for marinade.
3. Place sirloin in pan, and pour on marinade; marinate 1-2 hours.
4. Remove, grill 15 minutes each side, basting frequently with marinade.
5. Do not overcook. The meat will have a rare appearance due to the absorbed marinade.
6. To serve, crosscut on grain.

Serves 6-8

SOUTHWEST

Hacienda Frijoles

1 (2 pound) package pinto beans	1 (16 ounce) can chopped tomatoes
Water	1 cup barbecue sauce
2 teaspoons salt	1 (4 ounce) can chopped green
2 large onions, chopped	chilies, drained
2 cloves garlic, minced	1/4 teaspoon cumin
	1/2 teaspoon pepper

1. Rinse beans under cold running water.
2. Place in large kettle, and cover with cold water 2 inches above beans. Add salt; bring to a boil.
3. Lower heat and simmer, covered, 1 hour.
4. Stir in onions, garlic, tomatoes, barbecue sauce, green chilies, cumin, and pepper until well blended; return to boil.
5. Lower heat and simmer until beans are tender, about 1 hour.

Serves 8

STEAK TIP: For steaks at least 1/2-inch thick, you will want to sear them on each side for about 90 seconds in order to seal in the meat's natural juices.

Steak Tino

Grande
Beef Burgers

Colorado Department of Agriculture

Grande Beef Burgers

Here's What You Need!

1 pound ground beef

1 teaspoon ground cumin

1 teaspoon salt

1 (4 ounce) can chopped green chilies, drained

3 ounces Monterrey Jack Cheese, cut into 6 slices

1 round loaf sourdough bread

2 tablespoons butter, softened

1 cup shredded lettuce

1 small tomato, chopped

2 green onions with tops, thinly sliced

2 tablespoons sliced pitted ripe olives

1/2 cup sour cream

Guacamole

Here's What You're Doing With It!

1. Combine ground beef, cumin, and salt, mixing lightly but thoroughly.
2. Line 9-inch round pan with aluminum foil.
3. Divide beef mixture into 2 equal portions; shape 1 portion into large patty by pressing meat lightly but firmly into pan.
4. Remove patty and place on lightly greased flat baking sheet.
5. Sprinkle chilies evenly over patty; arrange cheese over chilies.
6. Shape remaining beef mixture into large patty; place on first patty.
7. Press edges together securely to seal.
8. Place burger on grill over medium hot coals.
9. Cover cooker and grill 7 minutes.
10. To turn, slide lightly greased flat baking sheet under burger.
11. Hold another flat baking sheet over burger; flip over and carefully slide uncooked side onto the grill.
12. Continue grilling, covered, 7 minutes or to desired doneness.
13. Remove burger from grill with flat baking sheet.
14. Meanwhile, slice loaf horizontally in half to form bun.
15. Remove soft bread from inside top half of bun, leaving 1/2- to 1-inch thick shell.
16. Spread cut sides of bun with butter; toast cut sides on grill 1 minute.
17. Place burger on bottom half of bun.
18. Arrange lettuce, tomato, green onions, and olives on top of burger; cover with top of bun; cut into wedges.
19. Serve sour cream and guacamole with burger.
20. If using an open grill, increase cooking time 3 minutes.

Serves 8

SAUCE TIP: Liven up your barbecue sauce by adding such spices and seasonings as chili powder, garlic, dried mustard, onion, Tabasco sauce, and even soy sauce.

Arizona Chili Sauce

2 tablespoons seasoning

2 tablespoons all-purpose flour

1/4 cup chili powder

2 cups beef or chicken bouillon

2 teaspoons salt

1 teaspoon garlic powder

1/2 teaspoon oregano

1/2 teaspoon coriander

1/4 teaspoon cumin

1. Heat shortening in saucepan.

2. Stir in flour; cook for 1 minute.

3. Add chili powder and 1/4 cup bouillon; cook for 1 minute.

4. Add remaining seasonings and liquid; simmer for 10 minutes.

Makes 2 cups

Southwest Margarita

1 lime, cut into wedges

Coarse or Kosher salt

1 (6 ounce) can frozen lime concentrate

3/4 cup tequila

6 tablespoons Triple Sec

1 (12 ounce) can lemon-lime soda

3 to 4 cups ice cubes

Lime twist for garnish

Lime peel for garnish

1. Rub rim of each glass with lime wedges; swirl glass in salt to coat rim.
2. Combine half of each of the remaining ingredients, except garnishes, in blender container; blend until ice is finely chopped and mixture is slushy.
3. Pour into salt-rimmed glasses.
4. Repeat with remaining ingredients.
5. Garnish with lime twist and lime peel.

BARBECUE TIP: Before using wooden skewers, soak them in water for at least 20 minutes before grilling in order to prevent them from burning.

Apple-Glazed Pork Kabobs

Here's What You Need!

2 tablespoons lemon juice

Salt, to taste

1 pound boneless pork loin, cut into 1-inch cubes

1 cup apple jelly

2 tablespoons lemon juice

1 cup cinnamon

1 tablespoon butter

Wooden skewers, soaked in water

Here's What You're Doing With It!

1. Sprinkle lemon juice and salt evenly over pork cubes.
2. In small saucepan, make glaze by mixing together the jelly, lemon juice, cinnamon, and butter.
3. Simmer until well blended.
4. Thread pork onto skewers and spoon glaze over all.
5. Grill over hot coals 10-12 minutes, turning and basting frequently.

Serves 6

Beer-Grilled Chops

Here's What You Need!

4 (1 pound) boneless pork loin chops

Marinade:

    1/2 cup soy sauce

    1 cup beer, at room temperature

    2 tablespoons brown sugar

    2 teaspoons grated fresh
      ginger root

Here's What You're Doing With It!

1. Mix marinade ingredients well.
2. Place chops in plastic bag, pour in marinade, seal bag, and refrigerate 4–24 hours.
3. Prepare medium hot coals on grill.
4. Remove chops from marinade; grill over medium hot coals 7-8 minutes
   per side, turning once.

Serves 4

Tex-Mex Chops

Here's What You Need!

1 tablespoon vegetable oil

4 boneless pork loin chops

1 1/2 cups salsa

1 (4 ounce) can diced green chilies

1/2 teaspoon ground cumin

1/4 cup grated Cheddar cheese

Here's What You're Doing With It!

1. On a grill, heat oil in heavy skillet over medium high heat.
2. Brown chops on 1 side, about 2 minutes.
3. Turn chops; add salsa, chilies, and cumin to skillet; mix well.
4. Lower heat, cover, and barely simmer for 8 minutes.
5. Uncover, top each chop with 1 tablespoon cheese.
6. Cover and simmer an additional 2-3 minutes, until cheese melts.
7. Serve immediately.

Serves 4

SOUTHWEST

Old San Antonio Barbecue Sauce

1 (16 ounce) can ketchup

1-2 jalapeños, chopped

1/2 cup Worcestershire sauce

1/4 cup tarragon vinegar

1/2 cup butter

Salt and pepper, to taste

1. Heat all ingredients together until hot. Do not boil.
2. Serve over beef or burgers.

Peach Cooler

4 cups cold skim milk

4 medium peaches, sliced with skin on

1/2 teaspoon vanilla

Dash of cinnamon

1. Combine all ingredients in electric blender, and blend until smooth.
2. Place in freezer 30 minutes.
3. Blend again and serve.

Serves 4

SAUCE TIP: You may want to create your own special homemade barbecue sauce by using corn syrup, molasses, or honey instead of sugar.

Jalapeño Marinade
For Chicken

1 cup jalapeño jelly

1 1/2 cups water

1/4 cup red wine vinegar

2 teaspoons dried sweet basil

1 teaspoon black pepper

1/3 cup olive oil

1. Combine jalapeño jelly and water; heat until jelly dissolves; cool.
2. Add remaining ingredients; shake until thoroughly mixed.
3. Immerse chicken in marinade 1 hour at room temperature, or 3-4 hours in refrigerator.
4. Barbecue chicken, adding additional marinade while cooking.

Makes 2 cups

SOUTHWEST

Texas Chili Dip

2 pounds ground beef

1 package chili mix

1 (8 ounce) can tomato sauce

1 (10 ounce) can Ro*Tel tomatoes
   with green chilies

1 pound cheese, cut into small pieces

Tortilla chips

1. Prepare meat and chili mix according to directions.
2. Heat tomato sauce, tomatoes and green chilies, and cheese in double boiler until cheese melts.
3. Blend cheese and meat mixture.
4. Serve very hot with tortilla chips.

Serves 12

Pancho Villa Dip

1 (16 ounce) can refried beans

2 jalapeno peppers, chopped

1/2 cup chunky salsa, mild or hot

1 cup grated Monterey Jack cheese

1. Mix ingredients together .
2. Serve hot or cold.

Makes 2 cups

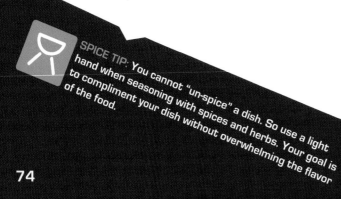

SPICE TIP: You cannot "un-spice" a dish. So use a light hand when seasoning with spices and herbs. Your goal is to compliment your dish without overwhelming the flavor of the food.

High Plains Chicken

Here's What You Need!

High Plains Chicken

1 cup French vinaigrette

1/2 cup white wine

1 cup water, or increase white wine

1 tablespoon roasted garlic and vinegar mustard

1 1/2 pounds chicken breasts

Here's What You're Doing With It!

1. Blend the first 4 ingredients well.
2. Place chicken in a shallow pan; pour sauce over the chicken.

Grilled Catfish with Hill Country Marinade

Grilled Catfish with Hill Country Marinade

Here's What You Need!

6 catfish filets

Marinade:

    1 tablespoon garlic, minced.

    2 teaspoons minced basil or cilantro

    1 cup safflower oil

Here's What You're Doing With It!

1. Mix marinade and soak filets for 1 hour.
2. Remove filets from marinade to hot grill.
3. Grill for 4-5 minutes on each side, being careful not to overcook.
4. Salt and pepper lightly.

Serves 6

Barbecue Fish Grill

Here's What You Need!

6 fish filets

Vegetable oil

1 teaspoon salt

2 tablespoons sweet wine

1 bottle barbecue sauce

1/2 cup minced celery, sautéed

1/4 cup slivered almonds

1/4 cup minced green onions, for garnish

Here's What You're Doing With It!

1. In a bowl, mix wine, barbecue sauce, celery, and almonds.
2. Place fish filets on grill.
3. Baste fish with marinade mixture.
4. Grill filets on low heat. Turn fish once.
5. Continue to baste heavily with marinade mixture.
6. Grill over low heat until fish flakes.
7. Garnish with onions.

Serves 6

SOUTHWEST

MARINADE TIP: Use roughly 1 to 2 cups of marinade for every 1 1/2 to 2 pounds of meat. The marinade should completely surround the meat.

Apricot Glazed
Pork Kabobs

Oregon Fryer Commission

Apricot Glazed Pork Kabobs

Here's What You Need!

1 pound boneless pork loin, cut into
  1-inch cubes
1 (10 ounce) jar apricot preserves
4 tablespoons orange liqueur, or
4 tablespoons frozen orange juice
  concentrate
2 tablespoons butter
Worcestershire sauce
Vegetable Options:
  Parboiled red new potatoes, cubed
  Mushrooms
  Cherry tomatoes
  Red or yellow bell peppers, cubed

HOME RUN

DIPS ★ SAUCES ★ BEVERAGES

WEST

Here's What You're Doing With It!

1. Stir together apricot preserves, orange liqueur, and butter.
2. Simmer in a small sauce pan until butter is melted.
3. Place pork cubes in heavy plastic bag; pour 3/4 cup apricot over to coat. Marinate at least 30 minutes in ice chest.
4. Thread pork onto 4-6 skewers. If using bamboo skewers, soak them in water for 20 to 30 minutes before using.
5. Grill over hot coals 10-12 minutes, turning occasionally.
6. Baste often with the marinade.
7. Warm remaining apricot sauce to serve alongside kabobs if desired.
8. Grill vegetables and pork on separate skewers. Vegetables and meat don't always get done at the same time.
9. Brush vegetables with some Worcestershire sauce while they grill.

Serves 4

BARBECUE TIP: Control the flames on a barbecue grill by having a pint spray bottle of water mixed with 1 teaspoon baking soda.

Grilled Lamb Chops Dijon

Here's What You Need!

3 tablespoons orange zest, minced

3 tablespoons fresh thyme leaves

3 tablespoons lemon juice

1 teaspoon cayenne pepper

2/3 cup Dijon mustard

4 teaspoons light brown sugar, packed

12 small loin lamb chops, trimmed of fat

Salt and pepper, to taste

Here's What You're Doing With It!

1. In a large bowl, mash orange zest and thyme into paste with back of spoon. Stir in mustard and brown sugar. Let stand at room temperature 1 hour.

2. Preheat grill. Lightly brush one side of lamb chops with about 1/4 of the mustard mixture, dividing it evenly.

3. When fire is hot, lay chops on rack, mustard side down. Cover and grill for 2 minutes.

4. Brush top of chops with 1/4 of mustard, turn, cover, and grill for another 2 minutes.

5. Brush and turn chops twice more and grill until mustard mixture is used up, about 10 minutes total grilling time for rare, or until done to your liking.

6. Season with salt and pepper.

Serves 4

California Cheesecake

1 cup finely crushed tortilla chips

3 tablespoons melted margarine

2 (8 ounce) packages cream cheese, softened

2 eggs

1 (8 ounce) package Monterey Jack cheese, shredded

1 (4 ounce) can chopped green chilies, drained

1 cup sour cream

1 cup chopped yellow or orange bell pepper

1/2 cup green onion slices

1/2 cup tomatoes

1/4 cup pitted ripe olive slices

1. Combine chips and margarine; press into bottom of 9-inch pan.
2. Bake in 325-degree oven for 15 minutes.
3. Beat cream cheese and eggs at medium sped until well blended.
4. Mix in shredded cheese and chilies, and pour over crust.
5. Bake 30 minutes.
6. Spread sour cream over cheesecake.
7. Loosen cake from rim of pan, and cool before removing rim.
8. Chill and top with remaining ingredients before serving.

Makes 16-20 servings

WEST

GRILLING TIP: Coating a chicken with a little oil or marinade prevents it from drying out while cooking.

Hot Spiced Cider Chicken

Here's What You Need!

2 fryer chickens, cut into halves	1/4 cup honey
1 cup apple cider	1/2 teaspoon salt
1 cup applesauce	1/2 teaspoon cinnamon
1 ounce cinnamon-flavored Red Hots	1/4 teaspoon nutmeg
1 tablespoon apple vinegar	1/4 teaspoon ground cloves
1/2 cup walnuts, finely ground	1/4 course ground black pepper

Here's What You're Doing With It!

1. Combine the cider, applesauce, and Red Hots in a sauce pan, and cook over medium heat on the grill until Red Hots are melted.
2. Remove from heat, and add the remaining ingredients.
3. Place the chicken halves on grill, and cook over medium heat.
4. Start basting chicken during the last 20 minutes of cooking time.
5. Remove chicken from grill when done (internal temperature of 180 degrees).

Serves 4

Mimosa

1 ounce orange juice

2 ounces champagne

1 ounce Chambord liqueur

Strawberries

1. Pour Chambord liqueur and orange juice into a tall flute.

2. Add champagne.

3. Add a strawberry to garnish.

Serves 1

California Barbecue Rub

1/2 cup cane sugar

1/4 cup onion salt

2 tablespoons seasoned salt

2 tablespoons garlic salt

1/4 cup paprika

1 tablespoon chili seasoning

1 tablespoon lemon pepper

2 teaspoons rubbed sage

1 teaspoon dried sweet basil

1 teaspoon dried crushed rosemary

1/2 teaspoon cayenne

1. Combine all of the ingredients, and blend well.

2. Store in a cool dark place in an airtight container.

Makes about 16 ounces

MARINADE TIP: Use roughly 1 to 2 cups of marinade for every 1 1/2 to 2 pounds of meat. The marinade should completely surround the meat.

Pacific Rim Burger

Here's What You Need!

2 tablespoons honey Dijon mustard

2 tablespoons mayonnaise

2 tablespoons sour cream

1 pound ground beef

2 tablespoons Worcestershire sauce

1 1/3 cups fried onions, divided

1/2 teaspoon garlic salt

1/4 teaspoon ground black pepper

4 hamburger buns, split and toasted

1/2 small avocado, sliced

1/2 cup sprouts

Here's What You're Doing With It!

1. Combine mustard, mayonnaise, and sour cream; set aside

2. Combine beef, Worcestershire sauce, 2/3 cup friend onions, and seasonings. Form into 4 patties.

3. Grill over high heat until juices run clear.

4. Place burgers on rolls. Top each with mustard sauce, avocado slices, sprouts, and remaining onions, dividing evenly.

Serves 4

Chili-Cheese Burger

Here's What You Need!

1 pound ground round

1 cup chopped seeded plum tomato

1/4 cup minced fresh cilantro

1 tablespoon chili powder

2 teaspoons minced seeded jalapeno pepper

1/2 teaspoon salt

1/2 teaspoon dried oregano

1/2 teaspoon ground cumin

1/4 teaspoon pepper

4 (3-4 ounce) slices Monterey Jack cheese

1/4 cup fat-free sour cream

4 hamburger buns

4 iceberg lettuce leaves

8 (1/4-inch-thick) slices tomato

Grilled onions, optional

Here's What You're Doing With It!

1. Combine first 9 ingredients in a bowl; stir well.

2. Divide mixture into 4 equal portions, shaping into 1/2-inch-thick patties.

3. Place patties on grill rack and grill for 6 minutes on each side, or until done.

4. Place 1 cheese slice on top of each patty; cover and grill an additional minute, or until cheese melts.

5. Spread 1 teaspoon of sour cream over top half of each bun, and set aside. Place patties on bottom halves of bun; top each with lettuce, tomato, onions, if desired, and top half of the bun.

Serves 4

GRILLING TIP: Never use a fork to turn the meat since it will punch holes and allow the natural juices to escape, causing the meat to lose flavor and become chewy.

Pacific Rim Burger

Pacific Northwest Barbecue Association

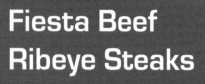

Fiesta Beef Ribeye Steaks

Washington Asparagus Commission

Here's What You Need!

4 beef ribeye or boneless top loin steaks, cut 3/4-inch thick (about 2 pounds)

2 tablespoons fresh lime juice

1/2 cup shredded Colby or Monterrey Jack cheese

8 medium flour tortillas

1 cup salsa, hot or mild

Here's What You're Doing With It!

1. Sprinkle beef steaks with lime juice. Place steaks on grid over medium, ash-covered coals.
2. Grill ribeye steaks, uncovered, 6 to 8 minutes (top loin steaks 10 to 12 minutes) for rare to medium doneness, turning occasionally.
3. Top steaks with cheese.
4. Serve with tortillas and salsa.

Serves 4

Grilled Asparagus

1 bunch asparagus

2 tablespoons olive oil

Salt and pepper, to taste

1. Trim bottom of asparagus.
2. Lightly brush spears with olive oil.
3. Grill over medium heat, turning once, for 3 minutes.
4. Grilling intensifies flavor of asparagus.
5. Can be used as an appetizer or served alongside your favorite grilled steak, chicken, seafood, or pork dish.

Jalapeño Cream Cheese Dip

1 (5.5 ounce) jar jalapeño jelly
1 (8 ounce) brick cream cheese
Tortilla chips

1. Pour jalapeño jelly over brick of cream cheese.
2. Serve with chips.

Makes 16 to 24 servings.

Red-Hot Sangria

1 large bottle burgundy wine
Red Hawaiian Punch
1 lemon, cut up

1 orange, cut up
1 small bag, cinnamon Red Hots
1 small bottle club soda

1. Mix all together and refrigerate overnight.
2. When serving, pour over ice and, if desired, add fresh fruit

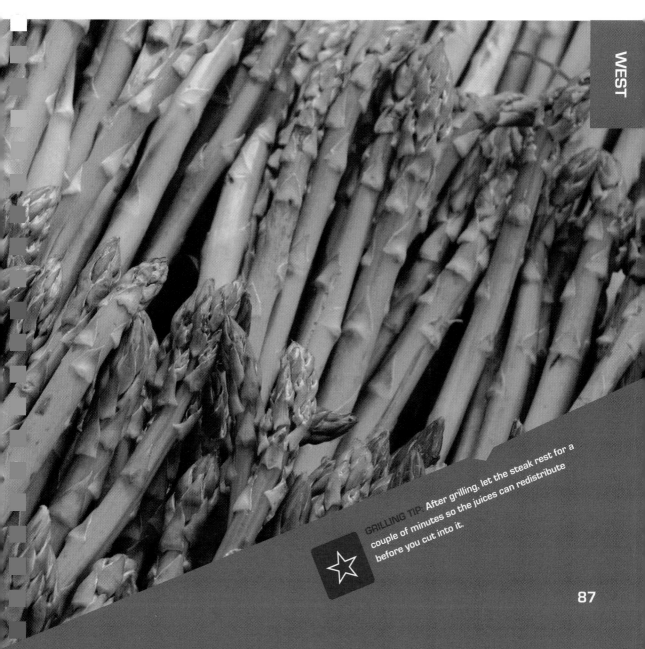

WEST

GRILLING TIP: After grilling, let the steak rest for a couple of minutes so the juices can redistribute before you cut into it.

Grilled Shrimp with Homemade Barbecue Sauce

California Salmon Council

Grilled Shrimp with Homemade Barbecue Sauce

Here's What You Need!
- 2 pounds uncooked medium shrimp, peeled and de-veined
- 1/4 cup olive oil
- 1 tablespoon minced garlic
- 2 cups bread crumbs, crushed
- 1/2 cup chopped fresh parsley
- 16 wood skewers, soaked in water
- Lemon wedges

Here's What You're Doing With It!

1. Mix shrimp, oil, and garlic in large bowl.
2. Add crushed bread crumbs and parsley, and toss until shrimp is evenly coated.
3. Sprinkle shrimp with salt and pepper.
4. Thread shrimp on skewers, and place on plate. Cover and refrigerate up to three hours before leaving for the tailgating party.
5. Prepare grill to medium high heat.
6. Grill shrimp until just opaque in center and crumb coating begins to brown, about 2 minutes per side.
7. Gingerly dip in Northwest barbecue sauce (Recipe below).

Serves 16

Northwest Barbecue Sauce

Here's What You Need!

2 tablespoons butter	1/4 cup onion, finely chopped
1 cup water	2 tablespoons Worcestershire sauce
1 cup ketchup	2 tablespoons lemon juice
2 tablespoons vinegar	2 tablespoons brown sugar
1 teaspoon salt	1 teaspoon dry mustard powder
1/4 teaspoon pepper	

Here's What You're Doing With It!

1. Melt butter. Saute onion until soft.
2. Add remaining 9 ingredients.
3. Simmer over grill heat for 20 minutes.

Makes about 2 cups of barbecue sauce

CAUTION: Never return cooked meat to cold marinade.

Plum Barbecue Chicken

Here's What You Need!

1 fryer chicken, cut into pieces

Pre-Grilling Sauce:
- 2 tablespoons soy sauce
- 1/2 teaspoon mustard powder
- 1/4 teaspoon wasabi powder
- 1 tablespoon sesame seed oil

Barbecue Sauce:
- 1 cup plum sauce
- 1/4 cup sweet chili sauce
- 1/4 cup soy sauce
- 1 tablespoon minced fresh ginger

Garnish:
- 1/4 cup mandarin oranges

Here's What You're Doing With It!

1. Combine the pre-grilling sauce ingredients, and brush on chicken pieces.
2. Grill on medium hot fire until almost done.
3. Combine all the barbecue sauce ingredients.
4. During the last few minutes of grilling, baste chicken liberally with barbecue sauce on both sides.
5. Garnish with mandarin oranges, and serve.

Serves 4

West Coast Sangria

1 bottle red wine

1 bottle 7-Up

1 bottle orange juice

1/2 cup brandy

1/2 cup Triple Sec

1 bottle vodka

1/8 cup lime juice

2 apples

2 oranges

2 grapes

1. Cup up all fruits and put into a large bowl.
2. Pour in all liquids, and let sit for at least 2 hours.
3. Serve over ice.

Chocolate Barbecue Sauce

1 1/2 cups ketchup

1/4 cup apple cider vinegar

1/4 cup dark chocolate syrup

1/4 cup olive oil

1 small onion, diced

2 cloves garlic, chopped

1 tablespoon lemon juice

1 teaspoon salt

1/2 tablespoon cracked black pepper

1 tablespoon paprika

1 tablespoon prepared mustard

1/2 teaspoon hot sauce

1. In a saucepan, sauté onions and garlic in olive oil, cooking until tender.
2. Stir in lemon juice, salt, pepper, paprika, and hot sauce.
3. Simmer for 5 to 6 minutes, and reduce heat.
4. Stir in ketchup, vinegar, and chocolate syrup.
5. Simmer for 15 to 20 minutes.

California Barbecue Association

GRILLING TIP: For steaks at least 1/2-inch thick, you will want to sear them on each side for about ninety seconds in order to seal in the meat's natural juices.

Ranchero Grilled Salmon with Roasted Corn-Black Bean Salsa

Here's What You Need!   4 fresh salmon steaks - six-ounces each

Here's What You're Doing With It!

1. Rinse salmon steaks and pat dry.
2. Prepare the Citrus Marinade.
3. Remove 1/3 cup of the marinade and reserve to add to the Roasted Corn-Black Bean Salsa.
4. Place the salmon on an oiled grill 4 inches from medium-hot coals.
5. Grill about 5 minutes on each side, brushing with marinade from time to time. Discard leftover marinade.
6. Salmon is done when the meat flakes easily and is evenly colored.
7. Serve with Roasted Corn-Black Bean Salsa.

Serves 4

WEST

Roasted Corn-Black Bean Salsa:

4 ears of fresh corn
1 (15 ounce) can black beans, rinsed
2 Roma tomatoes, diced
1/3 cup green onions, minced
1/3 cup cilantro, minced
2 Serrano chilies, seeded and minced
1/2 teaspoon chili powder
1/4 teaspoon ground black pepper.
1/3 cup Citrus Marinade

1. Roast the ears of corn on the grill until cooked and golden brown, 5 to 10 minutes; cool.
2. Slice kernels off the cob, and place in medium bowl. Mix in the black beans, tomatoes, green onions, cilantro, Serrano chilies, salt, chili powder, pepper, and Citrus Marinade. Stir gently.

Citrus Marinade:

1/2 cup fresh orange juice
1/4 cup fresh lime juice
2 tablespoons olive oil
2 garlic cloves, crushed
1 Serrano chili, seeded
  and minced

2 teaspoons lime zest, grated
1/2 teaspoon salt
1/8 teaspoon coarsely
  ground black pepper

1. In a small bowl, whisk together orange juice, lime juice, oil, garlic, Serrano chili, lime zest, salt, and pepper.

MEAT TIP: Season beef with sea salt and fresh ground pepper. The high mineral content brings out and brightens the iron flavor in meat that we all crave.

Ranchero Grilled Salmon Steak

Montana Beef Council

ULTIMATE FOOD GUIDE

1 Keep perishables, such as meats and condiments, in a clean, insulated cooler chilled with ice or cold packs. Place uncooked meat in well-concealed containers, making sure the juices don't leak.

2 Pack perishable foods between ice or cold packs. They will stay colder longer.

3 Keep nonperishable foods in a clean picnic or laundry basket, with the heavier foods on the bottom.

4 Pack foods that are already cold or frozen. It's not wise to assume that a cooler can cool foods adequately if they are packed at room temperature.

5 Keep hot foods hot and cold foods cold. Use insulated carrying cases with heated inserts to transport hot dishes. Keep hot foods above 140 degrees. For cold foods, bring enough ice to keep coolers below 40 degrees.

6 Marinate meat in a cooler or refrigerator.

7 Do not pre-cook meat on a stove or in a microwave before taking it out to grill at the tailgate party.

8 Remove meat from cooler immediately before placing on a grill.

9 Cook only that portion of the meat that will be eaten during the next two hours.

10 Use a clean platter for serving cooked meat since raw meat juices can contaminate cooked products.

1 BEEF • LAMB • VEAL STEAKS • ROASTS

Medium Rare
140 Degrees

Medium
160 Degrees

2 GROUND BEEF • PORK • VEAL • LAMB

PORK CHOPS • RIBS • ROASTS • EGG DISHES
160 degrees

3 GROUND TURKEY AND CHICKEN,

STUFFING AND CASSEROLES
165 degrees

4 CHICKEN AND TURKEY BREASTS
170 degrees

5 CHICKEN AND TURKEY,

WHOLE BIRD • LEGS • THIGHS • WINGS
180 degrees

**GUIDE TO
COOKING TEMPERATURES**